Talking Back
to the Moon

Robert Cohen

Traprock Books • Eugene, Oregon
2005

Acknowledgments

The Bathyspheric Review
Dream Fantasy International
The Portland Alliance
Fireweed
Spoon
Painted Hills Review
Portlander
Mr. Cogito
Rogue River Echoes
Messages from the Heart
Oregon State Poetry Association Newsletter
Writing Around Portland Newsletter & Anthologies

"Witness" received the Bob Simons Award of the 2003 South Coast Writing Conference.

"Your Sons" was honored by the Campaign to Free Mordechai Vanunu and for a Nuclear Free Middle East.

I would like to thank all Portland poets, the Bandon Writers, the Coos Bay Poets, Ron Levin & family, Mary Scheirman, and Ginger Andrews.

Talking Back to the Moon is published in an edition of 300 and sold by independent bookstores in Oregon.

Traprock Books
1330 East 25th Avenue
Eugene, Oregon 97403

Photographs: John Bauguess
Cover photo: Orchard Street, New York City
Book Design: Herb Everett, Peace Rose Graphics
Printed on 60# Vanguard Recycled Plus
from Living Tree Paper

ISBN 0-9714945-8-4

Table of Contents

Moon Madness

In Jamaica, they call it *Talking back
to the moon.* You can say anything:
counter-argue authority, berate your best
friend, tell a lover how unloved you feel.
And they can't complain, can't even claim
to be misused, because you talked to the Moon.
Who knows for certain what was intended?
Who knows it wasn't someone else of whom you spoke?
All that is sure is that you bent your head back
and brayed like a fool, and now you feel better.
And what harm can it do to the Moon?

In memory of my brother, Barry Cohen

For that which goes forth comes back changed
or dead.

—Conrad Aiken

Coming Home

Coming home, suddenly you appear,
a face in the window across the lost years.

The landscape has narrowed,
but the facts are farther apart—
scarred nearly beyond recognition,
or resurfaced like the cobblestones…

If you were here, I could remember
where to go—where the waffle-man rested
with his waffle-cart, and powdered
sugar clung to our sleeves like snow.

Arriving never entirely alone, never
together. Nothing gone but the time
to travel. And you always in every
window. And ever me coming home.

Father's Filling Station: A Photograph

By the radiance of his smile,
you can tell that he will fail.
No one treads that lightly on this planet,
or is illuminated for longer than a moment
before he flames out.

When the dream of a bright future failed,
he folded like a note
transferred from pocket to pocket,
tossed idly in the river
unread, just another sail.

Juju

The lamp that shorted out last week
lends an appropriate gloom
to the room where I sleep without windows,
painted police blue, with webs
in the corners where spiders can only wait
for other spiders to crawl.

And I lie in bed on my back
remembering Juju, the woman who once
tried to save me from myself.
But I was so cool—I was the blue
of this room. And the last thing I recall
is the sight of her legs leaving,
my good luck going down the hall.

Radishes

In memory of Harold Lawrence

1.
Has anybody here ever brought
radishes to a housewarming?
Harold did.
He said they made a perfect complement
to barbecued potato chips.
He also brought the chips.

2.
Harold loved Sally.
For her wake he prepared
food for a hundred.
Six or seven of us appeared.
We all cried over photographs
of Sally here, Sally there.

3.
I saw him last at the symphony,
poised above his cello, bow in hand,
attacking the Haydn on his music stand.
Black suit shiny over limp white socks—
that was Haydn, Harold-style.
Haydn rocked.

That Night

The air was cold, the walk was slow.
You wouldn't believe how the half-moon glowed,
though I learned that night to distrust aesthetics;
and how the heart makes history with its athletics;
and how the words that are left unsaid
leap from the shadows light-years later,
and assault you like the panther of your purest fear—
and leave you alone, and pure, and shattered.

You, Harriet Brown

It's well known that Greta Garbo
used a long string of aliases
to protect her anonymity,
best known of which was Harriet Brown,
numinous name of the girl I once loved,
perhaps still do.

Harriet, if you feel a faint flutter
down a forgotten corridor
in the high school of your heart,
have pity on a poor admirer
who's still sending valentines:
To Greta, wherever you are.

High Jump

When the bar is raised, it seems
impossible that you can clear it.
And even if you do, the bar
will only be raised higher yet.
Of course, you are one of the few
genuine prospects. If not you, who?
If not now, when? Yet as you hang
your arms limply and shake your hands,
visualizing your ascent, your risen
form, already you feel the animal
at your haunches, bringing you down—
predator earth, the ground of all ambition.

#2 Grief Point

This is where you go
when you can't go farther—
a bus stop without a bus,
Thanksgiving without dinner.

Later at Priest Lake I look
into the grief-gray water—
the whole world a prayer
that the world cannot answer.

Statuesque

Behind the museum, in the little park,
next to the statue of Stonewall Jackson,
I photographed you in an attitude
of mock defiance, a little general
though you couldn't hold the demeanor,
and we both collapsed in the grass
giggling and then grasping at bodies.

Were you ever photographed again
by anyone who loved you
half as much as I did then?

After you left—and still in my addiction—
I lost that photograph of you.
But I do believe that what I carry
is what passed into me
and what I pass on to others:
the memory of your statuary,
the grass and the flowers,
the little park behind the museum
held in a corner of my heart.

The Football Game: A Dream

See up there in the 15th or 16th row.
The girl I love is sitting in those stands.
A one-armed soldier is holding one of her hands.
Why don't I raise a cry? I try...I try.
I scream like a siren and wave my arms,
but football games are full of false alarms.

She's not pretending not to hear.
She's busy being what she dares to be.
I don't think that she'll look this way again.
(I can still smell her hair like a distant sea.)
The game is over. It begins to rain.
She's holding on to the veteran's empty sleeve.

Gray

for H.B.

You showed me the gray at the roots,
disappointed that age had an eye on you.
Siren of sighs, don't you know
that gray is the shade of the sea
and of sea-loving creatures?
Before I learned about oceans,
I learned about you,
true to your own seaward features:
mercurial darkness, a flash
of teeth on the wave, fin splitting
the water in a blaze of gray.

Her Summer Vacation

She returns from vacation abroad
with photos of what was left behind or lost
to a new term of teaching lost souls,
a new clutch of cohorts tossed
to the wolves of the new world order.
She wanted to teach for as long as she can recall,
but now it's just ten months from September to June,
and two months of trying not to remember
too much or too soon.
So she pours a tumbler of vodka before she unpacks
her clothes, and puts a disk on the changer.
She's listening to a samba; her eyes slowly close.
Maybe she'll take her winter break in Rio.
She can already feel the sand between her toes.

Slow Bus from the Coast

In the parking lot at Coos Bay, waiting
for the Greyhound, she's all hips,
driving her blond fullback
almost into the end-zone.

By Reedsport, she's returned
to the shore of the dying.
Little islet of indifference—
she doesn't even know I've seen her wildlife.

The Politics of Maureen

She leads me to a special place,
a garden tucked away in concrete.
I want to believe that here anything could happen,
anyone could meet his happiness.
Suddenly I take her hand, draw her to me, kiss
   her lips.
She tries to turn away, but she can't escape me.
Finally bursting free, she flees to the safety of crowds.
Soon she is lost in bureaucracy.

I caused this when I was in my thirties.

Riding Dad

You'd have thought on his broad shoulders I would ride
a king, unassailable from any direction,
unmitigated in the magnitude of my well-being.
But I thought that I would fall—that I
was in no way other than an ordinary thing.
So I tugged on the horn of his chin till his jaw
was sore, and he must have known for sure
the discomfort I was feeling,
for he set me down as though I were on my own,
and with no intent other than fair dealing,
we remained our own till he died—
the cut of that unweaponed wound never healing.

The Music Room: A Dream

We're at a lecture-demonstration by the great _____.
I'm seated at the rear, alone, attentive.
You're sitting in the center, surrounded
by friends and fiancés. The pianist plays,
the sound hard and brittle, bright and ringing.
I'm considering chords; I want to learn
the connection. I want to know
how things flow, and where they flow to.

Suddenly rude noises fill the air—the sounds
of laughter and love from around your chair.
The voices suck at my throat like a vacuum;
they're dredging my chest for a heart and other debris.
Do I turn with a finger to my frozen lips?
Do I demand an end to inattention?
No, I do not want to go on growing.
I, too desperate to make demands—I too
want to be rude, to forget in my own flood
the other flood that drowns me.

Reflections on the Current War

You might think it meant nothing,
that it happened merely by chance,
but this wave grew up on the other side
of the world, where once it was cradled
in a mother's arms, and rocked by a breeze
to the limpid melody of blue lagoons.

O love is not enough in angry seas,
and the gentle, if they are not crushed,
are coarsened, until like the surf they crash
on distant shores, the pride of a foreign
power, greeted by fools and feared by all
the wavelets orphaned in all the storms.

At Smelt Sands Beach

Dead mastodon of rock
driven from the cliff
to lie obliquely on a silken pillow,
trunk still uplifted: Did you appeal
to angels with your Gabriel-horn,
or were you just waving off a sniffle
when the sun set funereally—
the shore your tabernacle,
your desert the sea?

Her Boyfriend's House

The poster in the living room
read *Boredom is reactionary.*
I could love her anyway,
they're not her walls.

But how I'd love to hear her say
"Property is thievery."
I'd read her lips every day
with mine. We'd break down walls.

Mr. Cat and Me

He won't let me walk away
from the place where he waits
in the rain, uncomplaining,
with a tear that is there to stay,
like an orphan at the gate
in daylight's waning.

O something straight remains
in the bent and unbelieving
that won't let them walk away.
In the chapel of my brain
a family is grieving.
Then Mr. Cat comes in and I'm saved.

Witness

Before I wrote, I kept it all
inside. But it didn't fit—
I could feel the stretch and the bulge.
Finally, there was so much that it broke.
My tears were the blood of its objection.

Then, on a night of no mercy,
I awoke in a sweat and wrote it down
just as it came to me in dreams—
confused and intermittent,
crushing and palpable.

Now I wear it on my sleeve
like ink leaking from the pen I carry
everywhere I go.
It always knows that what seems easy isn't,
and it represents the risk I take
every day being free.

Writing is my witness.

No Go

You always knew you had to leave
to arrive. But whenever you stepped
through the door, a voice said *I'll die*.
The whole world beckoned,
urged you to reach far. But you only
circled the block, and went back inside.
You couldn't leave the voice that made
you finally round the corner and return
still unspent, undiscovered.
And now you only go as far
as the porch. And sometimes even
the porch is too far outside.
Then you sit and rock the chair,
and read the history you haven't made—
the book of your life a sum of blank pages.

Quicksand

for Sharon Doubiago

I don't know whether she heard it first,
or turned the fastest.
Then she was running through the woods.
The rest of us followed in fits and starts,
more casually than we knew we should.
The purest of apprehensions, alarm
is never falsely taken, though
its lack may be due to fear of failure,
fear of success, sophistication.
It wasn't quicksand after all,
just mud in the mind of a child.
And he was none the worse for a fall,
though quieter and muddier.
But she who ran when others walked
earns the star for special merit
on the report card of our lives.
Golden.

In Memory of Karel Ancerl *

You die with the prizes of your profession,
the statues and statuettes, plaques and mentions.
But no rest for the weary in their nation.
Again and again the tanks will turn toward Prague,
and there will be new bosses and new dividers,
and men will march to nearly any tune,
and the statues will crack and the mentions
    will not matter.

*Czech conductor Ancerl, a Jew, was the only member
of his family to survive the death camp at Auschwitz.
Long the head of the Czech Philharmonic Orchestra,
he left Czechoslovakia upon the Soviet invasion in 1968,
shortly thereafter becoming conductor of the Toronto
Symphony, a post he held until his death in 1973.

Brigade (Lines Overlooking Burger King)

The flag flaps like it means what it says,
but wind is cheap.
Finally, we are indifferent to its unfurl.
Just give the homeless a place to sleep.
Just give the world back to the world.

And mention us, mention us to your daughters.
And if you have no daughters, mention
us to your wives.

Woman Waving Good-bye

Beauty bends perfection
to the lived experience of a face.
That's why you read it like a poem,
memorize the way it smiles
from a platform at the railroad station
as the train pulls slowly from the gate.
And you turn halfway around in your seat
to watch a smile and a hand waving
until they are only memories,
a poem you recite silently
when the whole known world is gray and faceless.

Not Learning to Drive

I wanted to take lessons from you,
like learning to ride a bicycle in the alley,
not from my friends, with their own fathers waiting
anxiously at home for them to return
from their first evening on wheels.
I wanted to hear "As long as you're okay,"
in the wake of my first fender-bender.
But most of all, I wanted to drive with you
by my side, new license in my pocket,
along the winding road to Highland Park—
your slightly cigar-stained smile merely magic,
hair tousled by the wind, arm resting
heavily along the vinyl seat-back.
How long must I wait before we ride
along Lake Michigan by moonlight?
How long before this orphan son finds a dad
to teach him how to steer
the shore-hills of his life?

The Curve

In memory of Ed Dorn

There are some people who
once you look into their eyes
you never forget them.

He played a tape:
Someone was reading:
The curve of the universe is love

You could see the curve
of the universe
in his eyes.

Back in the Shadows Again

They've taken the televisions from the rooms
and the flavor from the food. The windows
of distraction are sealed and shuttered.
Lights out means life out, an interminable hiatus
for heads filled with desperate thoughts.
The lucky ones don't know that the new world
views them with disfavor, that they are the high-risk
pool, the corporate insurance adjustor's nightmare.

My insurance runs out all too soon—on the day
I am declared well, and sent home in a taxi
to sit in a chair before the television,
blinds drawn, enveloped in gloom,
in a cobwebbed room, on a sun-shiny day...
the sunniest day of December.

Mr. Cat and the Fleas

So much licking and scratching
has made him a hard-luck story.
One day an exemplar of upright living,
the next he looks like a loss of faith,
a lesson in broad understanding.
He curls on my chest and I'm stabbed
by a thousand itches,
as though a lifetime of indiscretions
had joined on my skin and risen
in revolution. I uneasily anticipate
civil war in the rug.

Wild Daisies

Because you grow where
nothing grows but grass,
and flash the smile
of the unaffected,
we love you already.

But that you mirror the sky
for a while,
wither and die,
makes you a wealth of beauties.

The Racetrack

for Moose

Because we were not yet old enough to vote
or to gamble away our wealth unwisely,
we attached ourselves to the nearest available adult
and entered the racetrack as somebody else's troubles.

We left, however, entirely on our own.
If any of us had change left in his pockets,
we all shared peanuts or ice cream cones.
Back to the darkened neighborhood,
the zone of disaffection,
our defeated families in their defeated homes.

Try again, try again tomorrow
to discover a soul
in the revolution of our blood,
to raise hope in the scrabble of vacant lots,
to pick the speed from a field of sorrels and roans
that only go once around the track,
and then they are winners or gone.

Your Eyes

Old ghosts on a gray day.
The last gossip of the leaves.
We danced a tango on the frozen ground of grief.
I never knew old knees could bend so deep.

You can't learn how to dance by watching feet
from a seat at the end of the bar.
These eyes are acts of war.
Your eyes are what they're fighting for.

Your Window: A Dream

I'm walking down Lincoln Avenue alone.
Past your apartment, past the porthole window
where we stood and touched, and where on a rainy
Sunday we watched a tug-of-war in the mud.
Your light is on; you stay up later now.
I try to turn away but I'm drawn to that light,
I bend toward that sun like a stem,
driven by a pulse I cannot persuade.

Suddenly you appear, framed in the window
like a photograph, a memory preserved
in myth, more real than real things.
I see you laughing; you're not alone.
You laugh and laugh, I never amused you so.
I can't leave. I can't go back home.
I have to relearn what I already know.
You turn the lights low. I wake in darkness.

Rope

In memory of Dave Levine

This is not fiber technology
or a history of the ties that bind.
This is a clearing in North Carolina,
amid thin pine and birch and alder,
and a rope around a branch that barely holds
thin Dave. He's spinning slowly in the breeze,
ecstatic, and the wind whistles a slow air,
and the leaves on the ground swirl
in a slow circle dance.

How he loved the accordion! He would play
the fastest dances and dance along.
His skinny legs would bend akimbo
as he pumped the bellows like no tomorrow,
and flailed the keys with breakneck abandon—
keys that flashed like the teeth of his laughter—
and faster and faster the dance and the dancer,
and closer and closer the branch of the tree,
and farther and farther the look in his eyes,
and tomorrow would bring no propriety.

After Celebrating My 49th Birthday

Say what you will to still the fear—
that I appear to be ten years younger—
this is the age that Father reached
before he couldn't reach farther.

He must have heard similar words—
I never saw him livelier
than before his heart broke of not enough,
and of trying to make not enough into more.

Cowboy on Stallion: A Photograph

It was only a half-gallon hat
on a half-pint head,
and only a burro pretending
to be a horse,
but I was Billy-the-Kid
for a couple of minutes
back in the summer of 1951,
when the photographer made
the usual corny remark,
and I almost smiled
who never smiled back then,
and he snapped the shot
which somehow came out dark
though the day was bright;
and I kept that photograph
in a box in the drawer
along with the cufflinks
I made in school but never wore,
until the time when I lost it all:
the dresser drawer, the box, the cufflinks,
the photograph of myself, age six,
shortly before Ma's first nervous breakdown.

Sitting at the Bar in Cassidy's Saloon

They want to drown my sorrows
in a shot of fare-thee-well,
a glass of see-you-later,
a handshake, and tomorrow
will be today all over.
It doesn't go away, it doesn't falter.
A habit is a reason not to change.
I lurch through the doors of ever-after
into the blinding light of yesterday.

Fishing Farwell Pier: A Photograph

I'm sitting on Farwell Pier, six years old,
a cane pole in my hand. I'm looking
toward the photographer—my father—

and squinting, apparently into the sun,
but really with that emergent self-consciousness
which would later become characteristic.

Also characteristic, I run out
of that photograph with the fish I caught,
run the whole way home to put that perch
in shallow bathwater, praying
for its revival—not ready to account
for the crime of survival.

Junk

When you go after it alone—
rehearsal for the role of not existing—
you become so small
invisibility would be a visible danger.
The wait in the parking lot,
without even a car,
and the rain isn't rain but tears—
heart of the junkyard dog.
Everyone talking about you,
the stranger in strange clothes,
who stands by himself next to a telephone
and talks without a voice
to a voiceless companion.

Click!

A door closes and with that click
the worlds of inside and out
are severed and fixed.

And love's image which loomed
like a drive-in picture screen
assumes its diminished position
in the reliquary of dreams.

Sleep

Giving up at least puts an end to trying.
Fernando Pessoa

To sleep is not to dream—
it's deeper.
That's why you fall
into it like a grave.
If it means anything at all,
if anything happens,
it's not sleep.
It must be opaque, immutable,
obeying the laws
of gravity and grayness.
It must be made of stone,
and stay. Anything less
and you are still awake.

Afternoon at Neahkahnie

for Suzanne

I'm sorry for what I said or did or left
unsaid, undone—whatever
caused you to turn away dispirited
and return to Springfield, Illinois.

But photographs from the Coast show you
pale and magnificent against a blue sky—
like Jeffers at Tor House gazing
solemnly out to sea—
archetypal.

Ghosts

In memory of Hyman Cohen, 1907-1956

1. The Afternoon Dad Died

I was at the museum with Ray and Sissie.
(Are you out there Raymondorino?)
We swore into acoustic shells,
and heard each other across a vast hall.
We picked up phones and dialed foreign
capitals, and swore in imaginary languages.
We watched little chicks hatch under the heat
of lights, and swore even though
the little balls of breath broke our hearts.

And when our money ran out,
it was three buses back to Rogers Park,
the warmth of three buses wearing us down,
through our pre-adolescent pretensions,
until we were three tired bundles
of childhood heat heading home.

And I said "Good-bye, it was great" to Ray
and Sissie, who turned right and left me alone
in the darkness of December afternoon, 1956;
and I walked down the block to 1734,
looked up at the luminous address
haloed by half-light behind the frosted window,
removed a glove and reached cold fingers
into my pocket for a key,
found the lock by feel and turned
into whatever I have since become.

2. The Chapel

His bosses, the Fenchel Bros.,
came in their matching black Cadillacs.
He who had died of overwork,
underpay, and lack of joy,
lay placidly before their gaze
while the bosses brayed about losses
and left as soon as safe.

Someone thought I should see him,
as though my dread were disrespectful.
I approached the coffin, gray
as the ghost of my father's face,
as the suit that he reposed in,
the only suit he owned—
he wasn't known for his clothes,
but for the amity that flowed
throughout the world he bestrode, a colossus.

What I felt was far, far away.
What I felt was alpha and omega.
What I felt was an alien in my nation.
What I felt was the dream where I had died.
What I felt was falling from a height
into a place where I was uncreated.

I returned to my seat, a mask of inexpression.
The rules, as rules will do, remained the same.
No one knew I grew into an exception.
I never mentioned the afternoon Dad died.

To an Editor

When you changed *lay* to *lie*,
it broke my lapsarian heart.
You punished the child for having a life
apart from you. Let him be his own boy.
Let him know the joy of music.
Sing to him when he settles in to sleep,
and sing to him when he awakens.
And if he rolls over again and closes his eyes,
let him lay or lie as he pleases.

Mr. Cat Gets Vetted

Mr. Cat came back with two things
missing, and I too am at a loss
for legitimizing concepts and just causes.
We sit by the place where the fireplace
would be if we had any fire,
and as he rambles in dream,
reviewing the orbit of ambitious youth,
I cast for words that would make the world over,
and whisper consolations for us both.

Unconditional Love

I planted English daisies and an apple tree.
Shirley insisted on a service.
Louis paid for a deli tray.
Her rabbi said you had a wonderful sister—
it must have been swell being you.
Your body was burned (you hated the word *cremation*).
I took care of Barry and business like you'd have
    wanted me to.

I flew back to Portland. That's when they came
in jackboots and kicked me down the stairs.
That was when my brain leaked fluid.
At the psychiatric ward, we sat in chairs
around a circle. That's when I wrote a poem for you.
I read it to the girl with razored wrists.
I read it to the man with Christmas gloves.
I read it to the woman who was blind from birth.
I called it *Unconditional Love.*

1957

I dreamed I met Annie Oakley
(not the one on TV).
She was tall and strong and handsome,
and she came all this way just to meet me.
We rode horses together.
Shot guns.
We were equals. Friends.
Before she left, we interwove arms,
branches from the same tree.
She said she would return, but she didn't.
Next year brought new leaves.

Your Sons

> *And boys, be in nothing so moderate*
> *as the love of man...*
>
> Robinson Jeffers

If they were mine, I too
would teach them not to overcare,
teach them even to be not wholly my own.
I'd sell them back to themselves and absorb
the losses. I'd have them disinherit the wind,
deny the weather, and turn into witless stone.

And still they'd be too human, still they'd bear
the scars of the hardening center like claws in the air,
the numbers on their wrists like yesterday's news—
like roadmaps to the mountains and the mountains, moved.

No claw, no crag, no breaker has
enough to say about the way we change
over and over into exactly what we are:
the human host preparing for the next war.

Black

Black as the flag of no nation,
the pavement winds like a ribbon
of grief, a reminder of dismal occasions.
I'm going back to Chicago.
I'm going back for a funeral holiday.
I'm bringing dark glasses,
cigarettes, a notebook,
two pens, and a pool cue
in a myrtlewood case.

Robert Cohen was born on the West Side of Chicago, Illinois, and raised in the North Side lakefront community of Rogers Park. He received his B.A. in English from Roosevelt University, his M.A. in Political Science from Northeastern Illinois University, and pursued doctoral studies in Political Theory at the University of Illinois in Chicago. He moved to Portland, Oregon, in 1990, where he worked variously as a writer and editor and as a residential advocate in Portland's homeless shelters. He relocated to Oregon's South Coast in 2002 to devote himself to writing.

John Bauguess of Dexter, Oregon, has been a social documentary photographer for 35 years. His work has included projects on homelessness, urban landscapes, living conditions of migrant workers and folklife projects, such as the Oregon Old-Time Fiddler Project and images of people displaced during urban renewal in the early 1970s. His work has been exhibited throughout the United States and published in numerous magazines. In 1996 the Metropolitan Transit Authority public art program awarded him an exhibition in the Lightbox photography gallery in Grand Central Terminal. In recent years he has switched from using traditional darkroom techniques to archival-quality inkjet print.